Animal Sizes

Contents **Page**

written by Pam Holden

A rabbit is a small animal.
It has very long ears.

Its back legs are big,
but its tail is short.

A mouse is smaller.
It has long whiskers
and a long tail.

Its tail is as long as its back.

A kangaroo is tall.
It has a thick tail
and long back legs.

Its front legs are small.

A horse is a taller animal.
It has long legs and a long tail.

Its head and its neck are long, too.

A giraffe is the tallest animal.
It has a long neck and long legs

It has small horns
and a short tail.

A hippo is a big animal. Its back is wide, but it has a thin tail.

It has short legs
and small ears.

An elephant is bigger.
It has large ears and
a long trunk.

Its tusks are long,
but its tail is small.

A whale is the biggest animal. It has a large tail and it makes a big splash!